# HIGH PRIESTESS

EFFIE M. KALAITZIDIS

**author**HOUSE®

AuthorHouse™
1663 Liberty Drive
Bloomington, IN 47403
www.authorhouse.com
Phone: 833-262-8899

Published by AuthorHouse  09/17/2020

ISBN: 978-1-7283-7220-4 (sc)
ISBN: 978-1-7283-7219-8 (e)

Library of Congress Control Number: 2020916722

Print information available on the last page.

For OA

# CONTENTS

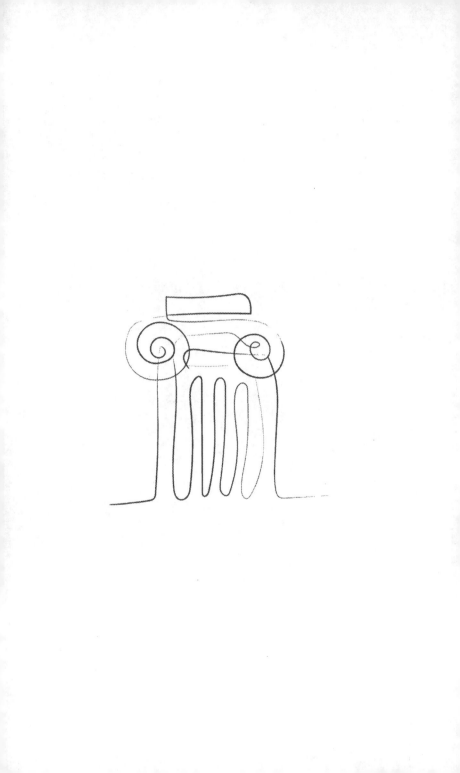

# QUARANTINE TAROT READING

Watching you burn the white sage we begin again the white minded meditation. We sit knees touching underneath the living room table. Legs criss-cross on the wood floor. The boards have creaked every night since I've slept on this couch. Cracking & calling attention to me. Sweeping me up out of mid-sleep like dust & dreams left to collect underneath. Like 4:11AM when Raphael woke me up, a hanged woman. Today is no different than others when the echoes of footsteps up the stairwell led to doors that did not squeak & swing open then slam shut. No fumble or jingling of keys. Scratching at keyholes to unlock. Just an end to them.

I stare down before me at the black paper & alphabet white writing, the ghost quartz crystal two fingers each touch. Like 4 of wands with the lazy dog beside us, ears perked at the ready for sounds of confirmation. Twin flame, past life lover perhaps, mirror image of my soul. Unspoken intimacy. A language we speak telepathically & through loving traces of ink born into our flesh the same day. A testament to the concept that we were birthed from the same star when created by source. A blip in the cosmos that led our life paths to cross. A catalyst. We were ready for a new direction.

We try to wake up the board by gliding the crystal across it mindlessly. The quartz slips through our fingertips & we utter quiet quick frustrations. We are being serious. You told me to ask it something & suddenly I have forgotten every intention of bothering the ghost in the first place tonight. My voice shakes as I ask if they were interested in speaking with us. Earlier this evening the cell phone went flying across the room interrupting our conversation. We had collected ourselves outside to speak in private. After months of oddities to connect. Now here we are & I am struggling to find the proper language to address the dead or the celestial. Pray to the archangels that the white light shield protects us.

Are you moving it? Am I? Have we synced wavelengths well enough to be guided at the same time? Radio static. I picture the telephone wires hanging outside my bedroom window & how the birds sit watching me dwell & over analyze my existence. The big black feathers that swooped onto my roof at the very moment my eyes gained sight after electric currents buzzed & kissed me awake at night. We hang up the line. I wonder how many times Hughes persuaded Plath to continue to try before they got it right.

I regain my focus as you bring out the tarot deck. You begin to shuffle the cards & I lower my eyes to search for a new channel of communication. These skills were developed from basic instincts I had known from my childhood games of psychic wisdom & levitation but have since chalked up to just an overactive imagination. It wasn't until we had met that I had learned of multiple dimensions, dreamscapes, & guardian angels. Suddenly my inner notions made sense.

I've spent the past few weeks in isolation growing my roots deep into the Earth in hopes that my healing could be a contribution to her healing as well. The night of the full moon in Libra, silver flowers grew from my crown as moonlight poured into my open chakras. I remember the vision from my meditation when I was shot up to the moon through the sky. I sat on top of her & saw the Earth through her eyes. The moon no longer in sight I realized I was her. You told me you knew it all along. I wish you knew how to swim.

3 of wands, 8 of pentacles, & the fool reversed. Drawn from the top of the deck you shuffled & cut. We are writers. The spirit knows this about us. It also knows that deep longing to create. The demanding desperation. The creeping fear that the water will flow to the brim & the brim will not break & the paper will not take any ink. The haunting of dry pages before us. We asked if they would like to collaborate, in hopes that we won't have to be responsible for every bright idea. Lights get heavy & too hot to hold & we are still holding on to our nerves. The spirit is asking us to free up our hands. To let go.

I close my eyes & listen to your clumsy shuffling. Swords & cups slapping & spilling into place. I find my loud voice & plug into the speaker box that sits behind my third eye's temple. I ask what messages the spirit has for us. I force my ego to shut up as I feel the white light pulse & send waves through the tiny stars & neurons that fire up my brain. I imagine your hands. The long shape of your fingers & the square of your wrist & up into the black orange blossom ink on your arm. I sit on my favorite leaf. As soon as I nestle there you draw. Page of wands, ace of cups, & the high priestess. This confirmation. Psychic powers are being tapped into. The high priestess is ruled by the moon & the moon is ruled by the chariot which is ruled by the smallest dimmest constellation in the night sky, Cancer, which rules my heart.

...

# SOHO

Just me & you
& the ghost in our hotel room

-Take these blue ones,
Let's play with magic &
I'll wear your T-shirt to bed

-Tie a red string
So you can find me.

The moon caught me looking again.

# 6 OF CUPS

Your tan skin,
The blue eye,
I'm greedy for you
My peace of mind
The storm won't break
As long as we sit outside
You're what hangs off of every sigh
I paid the stars to dance for us
Just to see you smile
A thousand lifetimes of longing
Let's not fuck up this time
Fated love / are you faded enough?
I told the moon that you're mine
Fill our lungs
Touch your warm skin
All the black lines
12:22
Sent from heaven
Our angels playing nearby

# THE LOVERS

A higher love
Let's get higher love
Electric when I'm close to you

No more hiding love
This is the kind of love
You buy a one way ticket to

# BANISHING SPELL

The record is skipping
While I'm trying to keep my voice down
Shakey with my matches
I've had to light the candle twice now
Kill the martyr
Matters in my steady hands now
Oh I think it's working
Call all my friends from heaven to come down
11:11
Oh you're just being funny now
Let's take a walk
My heels on the pavement are too loud
Follow the Moon down
I swore I saw her smile now
Kill the martyr
I'm The Star now

# 2:22 PM

I'll keep you like this in my mind
The clocks have stopped working
Let's reinvent time
Hide away in our own paradise
It's almost too easy
I've never been more scared in my life
We don't even have to say anything
Reading each other's eyes

# 8 OF WANDS

We left
Beautiful & restless
With only 24hrs to borrow
We move in silence
Louis V & the velocity

Flew all the way to NYC
Just to spend our Sunday
No one moves quite like us
No, they don't understand it

We fell right back into place
Minds spinning with stardust
Spilled onto our streets in SoHo
We move like poets
Gabriel & Saint Laurent

& me
Backless in Wang
Your spine broke
With your cheek pressed
In between my wings

Woke up & welded 14K gold
To the heart on my sleeve
& you
Oh you

I held you all night
In your hotel bed in Bowery

# BEST FRIEND

You inch your body close to me
But never close enough

Can you hear all my electric thoughts?
Buzzing like radio waves through our silence

You're so cute when you're silent

You look at me
But never long enough
You know it would be too tough
To climb back out of green eyes

They all call me eyes
I watch you exhale
Ghost rings in the pink light

# LUCID

My fingers in your mouth
Kiss the space between your brows
I'm sweet on you

# YEARNING

Tell you to come over,
It's getting colder now.

You keep lighting my fires
Keep my mind busy now.

# 3:33 AM

I already know all the places I would kiss if I ever had to say good-bye to you.

# JAR SPELL

The stardust danced inside the jar
As the crystals knocked into each other
While we let our dreams get the best of us

The best of us
Written in silent prayers
Like when our hands find any excuse
To touch a little longer than they should

Someday should come soon
Like late Sunday afternoon
Like when we practice
Speaking through our thoughts

Meditation
You told me you talked to the Moon
& I worry she might of told you
All the things I say about you

Slipping in & out of dreams you sent me
6AM poet that you made of me
The stardust danced inside the jar

# RETROGRADE

I left it all on the table
The bowl I packed still has weed in it
It's your hit

I could call your couch home
Today I hoped my sounds would wake you

So I could steal some morning moments
But I know you love to sleep in

Thought of texting you
But I let you sleep in

Smiled at the thought of you sleeping

Packed my suitcase on my floor
Time traveled all weekend
You met me at terminal 5D

You know our love is astronomical
Another time in space shit
Blame it on Mercury retrograde
Crying in my Uber home

# 5:55 AM DEN-ORD

I stayed up all night talking to my angels about you,
I told them everything I would never dare say to you-

What could I even say?

The fire you started still burns in the corner of the room.

# 5 OF CUPS

I don't get cold anymore
Oh Chicago you made me
& one day
You'll wish you would of kissed me
A little slower

# 10 OF SWORDS

I don't trust these ghosts
& they don't trust me

The living ones are worse
Than the ones that visit me

They don't creek the floorboards at night
They set fire to all my daydreams

Pirouette down like smoke from their attics
& wrap around the small of my back

&

Oh they make me bleed,
Ruby red
Because they needed me

# 6:66 PM

Do you mean the things you say?
Or do you just like the way it tastes;
On the inside of my mouth
In the dead of July,
I warned you.

# QUEEN OF WANDS

Poetry pokes holes in the velvet black sheet
to let light beams paint a better picture

A constellation of formulated truths
so as to make heartbreak sounds a little prettier.

I don't want to keep writing about this like most people
don't want to continue seeing their psychiatrist.

& yet we still need our meds
so here we are with the pen to the paper again

Trying to get our fix

# KING OF SWORDS

I give you a Libra pass all too often.
I spent months waiting for you to make a decision
that you were never going to make.

Somewhere in that big strong castle you've built in the sky
Where you hide under palms
besides pools & smoke pulls
from the end of your skinny hand-rolled cigarettes

I know behind your eyelids you're sorry
I just wish that when my eyes held your gaze
it didn't feel like there was a partition
being begged to be rolled down

To let secrets that have been held hostage
in the back of limousine daydreams go

What are you so guilty of?
Is this paranoia, or intuition?
Do I just need to take a break
from smoking pot?

Why do I fear abandonment so much?
No use in wrestling with sleep
& your stupid ghost
when I could be my own peace.

I've gotten comfortable sleeping alone in my bed

# 12:34 AM

Clumsy with my heart
I'm sorry I loved you too soon
Spoiled it like milk left out for weeks
On countertops
Spilled down onto
Kitchen tiles
When I realized
I was no longer your muse

# 2 OF PENTACLES

He never preferred women
So I decided to be art

# NO. 8

Its humid like
Green lights
So loud
LSD
The skyline

Let my hair air dry
Said you want to see it big

Like a lioness mane
Like some sort of Greek nymph
A goddess myth

Green eyes

& my venus is in Leo so get me right

# JUPITER

Got my highest self high
because she likes to get high.
Before I fall asleep
I kiss the moon goodnight,
& the night sky
& the bright pearly planet Jupiter,
who has been watching me sleep
for the past 3 weeks & is acting
like I don't notice him.
I was shocked
at the bright-white light ball
beaming in through my big sky window.
First at 2 AM in the throws of hot blankets
too hot
then feet too scared
of the dark
to be left uncovered.
At 5:11 AM
when I wake & see he is still beaming.
Patiently waiting for my attention.
I finally give in & meet his gaze.
I wonder if I've simply copied & pasted this glowing orb from
    my meditation visuals.
It looks like my God.
Speaking to it softly in the morning blue light, before the sun
    rudely interrupts us.
Jupiter is shocked when my full lips land sweetly on his cheek.
His shoulder.

He does not know a warmth like mine.
So far off in the solar system he rarely visits with the celestial
    beings of my kind.
Souls in bodies,
Angels in bodies,
what am I?
Born on a new moon in hot July.
Star seed.
I tell Jupiter I must have come unpinned
from the blue-black velvet
that drapes the scene outside
his own bedroom window.
Like a tiny pearl come undone
The angels must have seen me spinning
& flying fast through the universe's deep sea.
Now looking at you sideways
from the side of the bed I lay in
I'm feeling paranoid
that I am exactly where I am meant to be.
But the fighting rebel in me has softened lately.
Even the softest bits of my being have somehow
become softer.
Gentler.
For the first time I feel at ease
in my earthly body.
Your presence is strong but my intuition
tells me I have manifested this feeling
on my own.
You look at me like you see me.
& yet I can't tell if you're even looking at all.
You wake me up early

& keep me up too late.
I have not had an appetite for days.
You leave gifts at my door.
Black feathers.
Your gestures do not go unnoticed
when I have looked at the time
several moments past & it has not changed.
Synchronicities.
We speak the language of the universe.
You show me things I have forgotten
about myself or was too tired
to try to understand in
the heat of all the hot heartbreak.
I was besides myself.
Spring awakening.
You held my hand through the 444 portal
& watched as I walked through
the big silver arches in the sky.
Hugged my loved ones one by one
& met myself for the first time
As we embraced Uriel solders the edges
that separate us to seal in gold.
The next day
I saw the light you preach of in my eyes.
I think you just like when I write about you only.
That's why you persist that I write.
I anointed the pen so I could acquire
divine inspiration.
You agreed it would be best.
I started my meditations again
so I could try to hear you clearer.

You sent birds instead.
Beautiful black ravens
that watch me struggle for breath as I run.
Biting back the pain of fresh blisters reopening again
burning hot at my ankles.
You send me angels.
Cherubs
that tug & pull at the ends of my hair
& try to make me laugh.
You think I've become too serious.
You sent Michael to keep a closer watch on me.
He sits on the roof with my unnamed guardian.
I wonder what they do to pass the time.
Jupiter
what if you are not Jupiter after all?
How embarrassing.
You tell me what I call you doesn't matter.
Is this unconditional love?
I will never forget
the first time I saw you.
I remember thinking,
Why,
Has it been so long?
Surrender to divine timing
& you'll see
what's been there all along.

# BIRTHDAY(CHART) POEM

I was born on the new moon
the 8<sup>th</sup> day of July
I write poems like these
When the air is thick & hot
& the gray sky begins to cry

Downpour
I'm a sag rise
Hips & thighs
I rehearsed every sigh

My love is performance art
Get a little uncomfortable around Gemini
There's too much of it in my chart

& the moon & I
We are one & the same
Mermaid
Shapeshifter
God energy

You watch me fall apart
Just to piece myself back together again
& make a wish on me
Fly your spaceships & bring your country's flag
Now you own me

I'm not a patriot
I've had to share my birthday weekend
With the country painted red white & blue
& its off brand
The aesthetic lives in everything I do

Hear the thunder
Its lighting hits the swimming pool
& there's nothing to do
Besides skinny dip through my
Dizzy waters
When I think of you

# WHEN TWIN
# FLAMES KISS

Angel

Your lips taste like belief
& astonishment

Warm

Something I'd imagine
A star would feel like

Something bright
Like your smile

I could die on your couch

Another kiss
& we took the power out

Lights flickered
Like that night in New York

Blackout

& it's all your fault

Angel

It's all my fault

# CHASER

Balenciaga shoe box
Full of all my love letters
& prayers
Sealed in lipstick kisses
For the angels
For the moon
For you
Gym bag full of tricks
Florida water
White sage
Rolled all my elements
& magic
Into the t-shirt
I stole from you
Just to feel like you
Packed into my suitcase
With only my best running shorts

Runner

I have to keep running to keep up with you
I made it to the city
& now my view is another building
& the phone won't stop ringing

Runner

But it's never you
Phone interview
Anxiety through the roof
But I stay shining
North Star

So you know where
You're running to

Runner

I wake up & feel as if
You just left the room
Tell me what we do in the astral
Why do you keep it just for you?

Smoke again
Keep my head in a loop
Asleep again
To wake up & write
More poems about you

# THE STAR

False timelines
Shedding
Gold & iridescent
Find their remains
Outside of your apartment

In the heat
Of midsummer
New skin
Thicker
Aphrodite

Praying that you'll find me
Praying that I'll find me

The lines are getting blurry
Born with the world
Already burning

& Saturn is spinning its rings
On my finger
Put them in my mouth
So I can see them

Now I can hear them
Lay the deception
On the floor with clothes
& poems I could never
Read outloud

The deliberate blink
In the emergency room
Fish hooks & wire
Thoughts so loud
I thought they could wake you

Close my eyes
& feel the blue glow from
The television in your living room

Searched for my name
Inside your prayers
Fragments of the truth

Venus shining off somewhere
Unaware

In the heat of midsummer
New legs
Mermaid
Out of water

Seashells & fallen stars
Dripping off my body
Chicago alley wind storm
Homecoming to shore

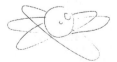

# AFFIRMATION

I am divine love
I am divine love
I am divine love

3 times in the mirror

I can fill my own cup
I can fill my own cup
I can fill my own cup

Without shame or guilt

I am divine love
I am divine love
I am divine love

Who would I be if I never learned fear

I can fill my own cup
I can fill my own cup
I can fill my own cup

Without shame or guilt

# ABOUT EMK

Effie M. Kalaitzidis was born in Chicago & raised in the northern suburbs of the city. Writing poems since the young age of 8 years old, she always aspired to someday publish her work. The effects of COVID-19 resulted in her losing her job as a professional make up artist & finding her life's true purpose. Through her spiritual journey she overcame blocks & self-limiting beliefs that held her back from pursuing her soul's desire. Spreading messages of light & love & helping others through their own spiritual discovery became her soul mission. While undergoing this personal transformation Effie began to share her unique talent of tarot divination on social media. Kalaitzidis became an overnight success on the popular social media platform Tik Tok where her tarot readings have reached over three million viewers. This exposure launched her tarot reading business EMK Tarot. Kalaitzidis lives & works in Chicago as an intuitive tarot reader & writes poetry in her free time.

Printed in the United States
By Bookmasters